STĀSTS PAR SKAITĻIEM

THE NUMBER STORY

SMALL BOOK ONE

ENGLISH – LATVIAN

Numbers Teach Children
Their Number Names

written and illustrated by

MISS ANNA

Early Reader Edition of *The Number Story 1*
Bronze Medal Winner, 2016 Wishing Shelf Book Award

Library of Congress Control Number: 2018902040

Names: Miss Anna, author.
Title: Number story : numbers teach children their number names / Miss Anna.
Description: Portland, OR: Lumpy Publishing, 2018.
Identifiers: ISBN 978-1-945977-33-6 | LCCN 2018902040
Summary: The pictures and rhymes present stories which introduce numbers 0-10.
Subjects: LCSH Numeration—English--Latvian--Pictorial works--Juvenile literature. | BISAC JUVENILE NONFICTION /
Languages: English--Latvian
Classification: LCC QA141.3 .M57 2018 | DDC 513—dc23

Publisher: Lumpy Publishing
Website: www.missannabooks.com
Email: missanna@missannabooks.com

Paperback: ISBN 978-1-945977-33-6
Printed in the U.S.A.   1 3 5 7 9 10 8 6 4 2

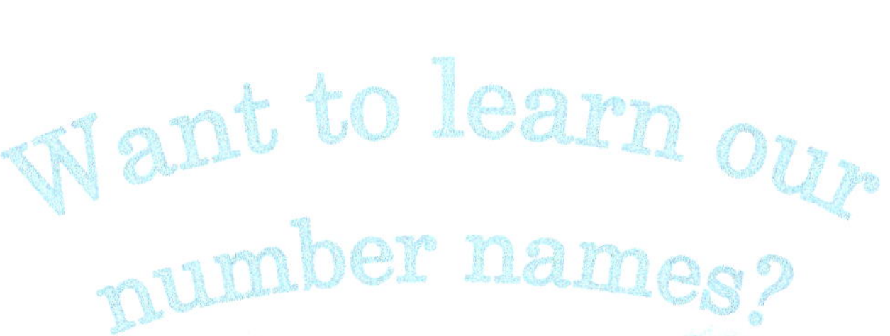

Vēlies iemācīties mūsu skaitļu vārdus?

It is very easy and a lot of fun!

Tas ir pavisam vienkārši un ļoti jautri!

Say-along our little jingle

Dziediet kopā ar mums,

starting from Number One!

Sākot ar pirmo skaitli!

1
ONE looks like my one finger.
VIENS
ir kā mans pirkstiņš.

ONE!
VIENS!

2

TWO trails a tail.

DIVI

ir aste.

A TAIL! ASTE!

3

THREE has bumps.

TRĪS

ir līknes.

BUMPY! LĪKNES!

4

FOUR carries a sail.

ČETRI

nēsā buras.

A SAIL!
BURAS!

5

FIVE   is a racing track.

PIECI

ir kā auto trase.

VROOM
BRR BRR!
1

S I X   curves like a snail.

SEŠI

ir kā gliemis.

A SNAIL! GLIEMIS!

7

SEVEN   has a sharp angle.

SEPTIŅI

ir ass stūris.

OUCH!
AU!

8

EIGHT   is rollercoaster rails.

ASTOŅI

ir jautrie kalniņi.

CIK FORŠI!
YIPPEE!

NINE is a bubble on a stick.

DEVIŅI

ir burbulis uz kāta.

A BUBBLE! BURBULIS!

10

TEN   is an eye of a whale.

DESMIT

ir viena vaļa acs.

WINK!

ACS!

And
Un

0

ZERO   is an empty pail.

NULLE

ir liels, tukšs spainis.

IT'S
EMPTY!
TUKŠS!

Thank you for playing with us today.

We had a lot of fun too!

Paldies, ka šodien ar mums spēlējies.

Mums arī bija ļoti jautri!

We are your Number friends,
Zero to Ten,
Who will be here for you~
Mēs esam tavi draugi skaitļi
no Nulles līdz Desmit
kas vienmēr būs kopā ar tevi~

Bye-bye now!
See you again soon.
Uz redzēšanos!
Tiekamies jau pavisam drīz!

The Numbers are *SINGING* too!

To sing-a-long, look for Miss Anna Number Story
at your favorite music store like iTUNES.

MP3

Numbers 0-10
IDENTIFYING
& COUNTING

Numbers 11-20
& Ordinals
first, second, third...

Numbers 0-100
& Place Values
ones, tens, hundreds...

About Clocks
& Telling Time
hours, minutes, seconds

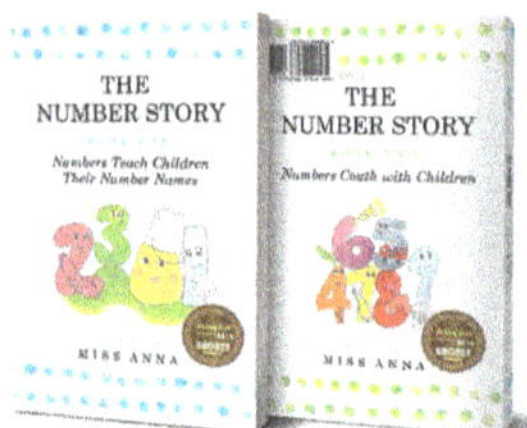

Number Story 1 & 2
isbn: 978-0-996216-48-7

Number Story 3 & 4
isbn: 978-1-945977-01-5

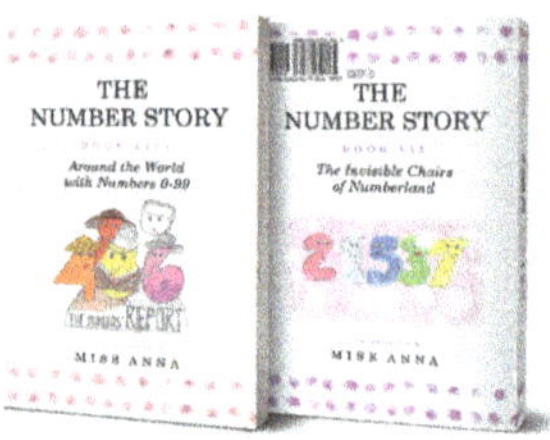

Number Story 5 & 6
isbn: 978-1-945977-06-0

Number Story 7 & 8
isbn: 978-1-949320-40-4

For more Miss Anna books to love,
visit us at

www.missannabooks.com

Numbers are working hard all over the world!
Come Travel the World with Us!